GW01425216

Keepsake

Kayleigh Campbell

Maytree Press 2019

Published 2019 by Maytree Press

www.maytreepress.co.uk

ISBN: 978-1-9160381-6-5

A CIP catalogue record of this book is available from the British Library.

Cover image: Reverie © Caroline Brown

Maytree 007

Printed in the UK by PiggyPrint

Acknowledgements

A heartfelt thanks to the editors of the following publications in which some of these poems have first appeared: Eye Flash Poetry, Yaffle Whirlagust Anthology and Peeking Cat Poetry.

About the author

Kayleigh Campbell, a Leeds based writer, is a Creative Writing PhD Researcher at The University of Huddersfield and also works as an Editorial Assistant for Stand Magazine. Her poetry has been published widely both online and in print, including The Butcher's Dog, Black Bough Poetry, Eye Flash Poetry and Yaffle Press. She was commended for the Geoff Stevens Prize and recently, shortlisted for the Streetcake Magazine Experimental Poetry Prize.

For Joe, for showing me kindness when I needed it the most.
And for Eliza, my greatest joy.

Contents

On being, a 40lb Pike

After 'On catching a 40lb pike' by Ted Hughes.

She started off slight, not a sign.
And so she swam,
and she swam
    and she swam
        and she dived deeper still,
to no-[wo]man's land,
where one cannot see
what sometimes desperately
lies beneath.
As she moved with the water
her skin stretched,
slowly but determinedly.
She caught glimpses of her growing body
in shards of broken glass
or plastic bags
glittering in the Spring sun
which broke through the surface.
She tried, every other day
to perforate the bulge
in the hope it's contents may
slither into nothingness.

To her dismay they were displayed
across the riverbed,
latched on vegetation, incubating.
Midday, early April
a five pound egg cracked
and she was overcome with melancholy.

Lindisfarne

Sand dunes guard the way to the water's edge,
whispering warnings as we pass each one.
They clutch at our feet, begging us to stay;
we leave them behind, face the open beach.
There are thousands of footprints, tracing
over each other, still harbouring the owner's warmth.
We follow them, in every direction.
The tide sashays in and out,
                                    in and out,
peeking at the lines in the prints, the patterns.
Seaweed like Serpents, waiting.
We stop,
see the Holy Isle like a siren in the sea.
It's causeway calls, like a portal.
My feet stick firm to the sand,
I cover my eyes with my hands.
The waves collapse,
heavy with tears of those who didn't make it.

Anxiety: Day 2190

There are lots of books to help
and motivational speakers
and therapists
and pills
and parents telling you to be happy
and inspirational quotes on Instagram
and group sessions
and adult colouring books
and yoga
and deep breathing
and sleep
and sex
and running a sink full of cold water
and

Birthday

The nurse, a gloved hand
and a sympathetic look.
Tremors continued to wreak havoc
on my body;
the Richter scale broken.
And you were still,
awaiting extraction.
Blood seeped from between my legs,
then came the shit;
infantile as I edged towards motherhood.
An audible pop
and the holy water came.
You followed, head first.
I looked out over the rooftops of the city;
your skin on mine,
strangers,
even after all this time.

He touched me here

The flies started that night,
in the kitchen that always felt dirty.
She counted thirteen.
She left them to their own devices
as she went back to sleep,
knowing that they would find a way to leave.
The next day she counted eighty-five,
not including the ones that lingered
under her skin.

Keepsake

One of the first things I bought for you
was a soft rabbit;
sweet, neatly stitched, delicate.
Now I can't stop seeing dead rabbits
on the road and in my dreams.
Matted fur, blood congealing on tarmac;
tissue and flesh scattered like petals.
The eyes still flicker though.
The rabbit sits on your windowsill;
I peek at it while you sleep.

Secondary drowning

It is the rain demanding you open the window,
it is the wind threatening to break you.
It is the bedroom door open and not closed.
It is the way the shadows creep,
the way the silence leaves you listening.
It is the yearning for morning,
the myth that light is your friend
and the dark is not.
It is the shortness of breath
amongst all the air in the room.

The day we ate at the port in Barcelona

You are sad again;
you are sad because of a boy.
The boy who made you feel special
because he called you handsome,
text first everyday, last to text at night,
made you come
for the first time outside your own hand.
You are wordless, vacant eyes
fixed on the turquoise ocean
next to our dinner table.
I push expensive lamb around my plate
in all its Red Wine infused glory.
Your loss is infectious -
I ache for a boy that isn't mine.

Test Tube

We kept the cord;
now shrivelled, blackness.
It's on the new IKEA bookcase.
Skin,
smaller than a ten pence piece.
For nine months we said we wouldn't,
rolled our eyes, turned our noses.
But your flesh is golden.

Bruxelles

Oh, we were so raw then.
Early winter,
exploring the insides of each other's pockets.
We laughed at the little pissing boy,
how underwhelming it was.
You gripped my hand tightly.
Colour fell from the walls
into our heads.
I took a thousand pictures.
The cold rushed us into a bar,
full of old men
waiting for someone, or each other.
We still talk about that place,
full of Saint Nicholas statues
and all kinds of love.

Postpartum

Do you remember what you said?
You said that you wanted me here,
so you could love me
and that would be all that mattered.
I could hardly move,
surrounded by tubes
darkness and fluids;
but I wriggled with euphoria.
I wanted to meet you too.
The one who sang Breakfast At Tiffany's,
treated me to Pain Au Chocolat.
Laughed at some hiccups.
But now you don't sing anymore
and you don't eat pastries because they make you fat.

Thank you

Since the beginning
I've always left blood trails
hoping that you would follow
to find what was bleeding.
You did, and you do;
only now I've taken to painting the walls
and staining the sheets.
You run water over linen,
re-emulsion every year
and fill vases with Tulips.

Six weeks and three days

Onions make you weep;
when you peel back layers
they start to seep.
Your eyes pucker then give way.
You keep slicing and slicing
until you can't see anymore.
When they peeled back the layers,
and sliced away,
I tried my hardest, but
I was actually elated.

Berlin

Her reflection captured in the aquarium glass,
like a seventies polaroid
screaming nostalgia.
Translucent blue,
exposed concrete,
flashes of yellow,
chalky white.
Off focus,
over exposure.
She stares at her reflection,
until she doesn't recognise her own face,
until the colours merge into one,
her eyes only blackness.
She's always waiting for him to appear,
swirling the chaos of colour
and despair.
But, this time
it is you she sees.
She takes a picture of you both,
and walks on.

Pret A Manger

Most days we saw your dad,
a stolen hour
in the same cafe.
Filter coffee and a coconut-milk latte.
We mainly talked of you
and sank into chairs;
another broken night.
I've never worn a watch,
but I could hear ticking.
Your dad would leave,
I'd be lost again
in a sea of people
where nobody looked like me.

Vanilla

Blossoms line the street like girls in
red light districts;
pretty, waiting to be admired.
March rain patters on our faces
like tears falling from our mothers
as they watched our features change
with age and experience.
Your eyes glaze with a haziness,
a boredom of finding
an extraordinary brunch spot.
We stop,
watch the blossom float onto concrete
and look on as the pinkness smears
into ordinary.

It was just one of those afternoons

You won't remember this day when you're older;
it'll be tucked into the past like boxes in the attic.

But I wish we could stay in this tiny room
with my travel books, your dad's Pokémon figures,

the Laura Marling vinyl I got for my birthday;
the first one you shared with me.

The chocolate chip cookies on the desk,
the rolls of wrapping paper that are too pretty to use.

The poetry, the pots of pencils and the black cat poster.
Your dad's old lamp that has bubbles inside it.

I wish you could remember how you smiled,
as tears were rolling softly down my cheeks,

and how sobs turned into laughter,
yours and mine.

A list to live for

My daughter's laugh.
Fresh Lavender.
The morning, specifically between 8am and 9am.
French Pastries.
New books.
Coffee with Irish Cream.
The relief after sneezing.
Walking.
Cinnamon-scented candles.
The way light falls.
His touch disappearing from my skin.

Childcare

It hits harder than a punch in the stomach;
my eyes fill with water.

Our mornings stick together
like strawberry jam clings to porridge.

Our evenings merge into one
the way the light succumbs to the deft touch of night.

You are debt-free.
You laugh at coloured stars on the tv screen.

You fall asleep in your food and wee in the bath.
You smile and our worries pause,

if only for a moment.
I want you to stay like this.

Baptism

People asked if we were going to Christen you.
Though my father believes in redemption to get to heaven

and that temptation keeps the path straight to hell
and though I can see the appeal of bodies

huddled together in pews each longing
for the same kind of belonging

and in turn belonging together,
I sin and I'm peaceful for that.

There is no man in my sky, only clouds
that darken then scatter like clockwork.

But here in this bath, as your dad
holds you to my breast

I almost go to sprinkle water
upon your newborn head.

The lighthouse keeper wanted to marry she

They are not lost at sea,
but stuck in a lighthouse.
Chasing each other up and down
a spiral staircase,
their shortcomings echoing around curved walls.
They take it in turns
to shine a light over ships in the distance;
momentary distractions
from holy matrimony.

Treading Water

An early morning in Lunenburg,
breath stolen in the still.
The sea luminous — turquoise,
peppermint green, mustard seaweed.
Our hands trace sketching on stone;
worn with time, like the best of us.
We circle rock pools
whisper our blueness like incantations,
hovering over hairline cracks
in water smoother than glass.

Patisserie Florentin

A young couple are sitting in a cafe.
He sips an americano, she's already finished her latte.

They eat rich, handmade brownies;
old ladies gather in pairs around them.

Antique decor; floral, faded wallpaper,
pictures of birds in cages, old postcards on the walls.

Little conversation, steam rising from mugs,
the radio playing to itself in the kitchen.

They leave,
stand in the morning sun for a moment;

cradling their bodies and their youth.

The first year

Darkest blue, deepest blue.
Sea blue and sky blue.
Lightest blue and shallowest blue.
Baby blue and baby blues.

Baby blues,

baby blues,

baby blues,

baby blues,

baby blues,

baby blues,

baby blues,

baby blues,

baby blues,

baby blues.

Baby,

I'm blue.

They brought her home

Ashes;
disappearing into the breeze
as the lilac swayed hauntingly
in Annat Hill.